LYUDMILA PAVLICHENKO

History Nerds

CONTENTS

Title Page
Chapter 1: From Student to Sniper   1
Chapter 2: The Sniper's Dilemma   11
Chapter 3: Who Feared Lyudmila Pavlichenko?   22
Chapter 4: Other Notable Mentions   40
Chapter 5: Comparison with Modern Snipers   44
Conclusion: Lady Death's Legacy   50

CHAPTER 1: FROM STUDENT TO SNIPER

Who Dares to Aim?

What drives a young student to trade books for bullets, aiming not for grades but survival? Lyudmila Pavlichenko's remarkable journey from academia to a sniper's hide raises this profound question. It challenges our understanding of courage, conviction, and the depths of the human spirit.

To grasp the magnitude of her decision, we must consider the context of Pavlichenko's life. She was born in 1916 in Ukraine and grew up during relative peace, dreaming of pursuing higher education and making an intellectual mark on the world. However, as war loomed over Europe, Pavlichenko faced a stark choice: continue her studies while her country faced an existential threat, or take up arms to defend her homeland and risk everything.

Many assume self-preservation would trump duty

or patriotism. But for Pavlichenko, the call to serve proved irresistible. She recognized the fight against Nazi Germany as a struggle for her nation's soul. Sitting idly while others sacrificed their lives seemed cowardly and a betrayal of her values.

However, we cannot paint Pavlichenko's decision as purely noble or selfless. Like anyone, she grappled with fear, doubt, and the knowledge her choice could lead to death. She had to weigh her dreams against her country's needs, knowing she might never return to her former life.

Perhaps her early sharpshooter training instilled a sense of duty to use those skills defensively. Or perhaps her deep love for her homeland made her unwilling to see it fall under Nazi oppression. Ultimately, she may have recognized history's moments when individual choices have far-reaching consequences, and shirking responsibility betrays one's values.

Of course, Pavlichenko could not have known her actions would help turn the tide or that she would become a celebrated sniper. She made her choice based on deep conviction and willingness to risk her life for something greater.

It's tempting to view Pavlichenko's story as an outlier with little bearing on our lives. But the truth is we all face moments to stand up for our beliefs or retreat into inaction's safety. Her example reminds us that individual actions can make a difference, even against overwhelming odds.

Pavlichenko's choice reflected personal values beyond military heroism. As a woman in a male-dominated field, she overcame enemies' bullets and comrades' skepticism. Her success proved women could be as capable and deadly as men in battle.

In this sense, Pavlichenko's legacy extends beyond warfare. She symbolizes individual agency's power and ordinary people's ability to rise to extraordinary challenges. Her story reminds us greatness lies within each of us, waiting to be unlocked through courage, sacrifice, and unwavering belief.

Of course, her path was not easy. She witnessed war's horrors, losing friends and grappling with killing's psychological toll. Yet she never lost sight of her purpose: her painful actions served a higher cause of protecting her country and people.

Reflecting on her feats as a sniper misses her story's deeper human significance. Her choice was profoundly human, speaking to the resilience and indomitable spirit of the human soul.

In a cynical, self-interested world, Pavlichenko's example inspires hope. Her story reminds us that even in darkness, some will stand for their beliefs and put their lives on the line. It testifies to conviction's power and the enduring human spirit.

As we navigate life's challenges, we can draw strength from her example, knowing even daunting obstacles can be overcome through courage, determination, and unwavering commitment to what's right.

Ultimately, the question of what drives a student to swap books for bullets defies easy answers. It speaks to personal conviction, societal pressures, and history's unpredictable tides intertwining. But in Pavlichenko's story, we find a powerful reminder of the human spirit's capacity to rise, leaving an indelible mark through actions and beliefs.

Marksmanship The Sniper's Lexicon

To truly understand Lyudmila Pavlichenko's transformation into a legendary sniper, we must first decode the language of her deadly craft. The sniper's lexicon is a dialect of precision, patience, and skill. Terms like "windage" and "ballistics" hold the keys to mastery. Decoding this jargon illuminates not only the technical aspects but also offers a glimpse into the mindset of those wielding these tools of war.

"Windage" might evoke gentle breezes to the uninitiated. But for the sniper, it represents a critical factor determining a hit or miss. Windage is the horizontal adjustment made to compensate for wind's effect on a bullet's trajectory. It reminds even the most skilled marksman that they are at nature's mercy.

Picture the sniper perched in their hide, watching the target through the scope. They must gauge the distance and read the wind like a sailor reads the sea.

Is it a steady easterly breeze or a gusting crosswind that could push the bullet off course? The sniper makes split-second calculations, adjusting their aim to account for this invisible force.

But windage is just one puzzle piece. "Ballistics," the study of projectile motion, looms large too. It encompasses factors influencing a bullet's path - velocity, weight, atmospheric conditions. For the sniper, ballistics is intimate knowledge, a second language spoken fluently. They understand how the bullet will behave, accounting for gravity's pull, air resistance's drag, even the Earth's rotation.

This ballistic mastery allows snipers to make impossible shots - arcing bullets over vast distances, threading through narrow opportunities. It blends technical prowess with intuitive feel, bordering on artistry.

The lexicon extends beyond technicalities to psychological dimensions. "One shot, one kill" encapsulates the sniper's lethal efficiency ethos. It reminds that each trigger pull carries immense responsibility - every bullet must serve a purpose.

For Pavlichenko, a woman in a male field, this likely held special meaning. Each enemy felled proved her worth, challenging doubters of her abilities.

Another key term is "camouflage" - blending into surroundings. For the sniper, invisibility is power, allowing prey to be stalked undetected. But camouflage transcends physical concealment; it's a mental discipline, subsuming one's identity into the mission.

Pavlichenko likely understood this deeply. Donning her camoflauge, nestling into her hide, she shed Lyudmila the student, daughter, dreamer - becoming a wraith, an instrument of war. Camouflage let her transform, abandoning individuality for a higher cause.

Finally, "confirmed kill" carries chilling weight. It verifies an enemy casualty, grim validation that deadly skills were used. But for Pavlichenko, it likely held complex significance. Each confirmed kill inched closer to victory, defending her country - yet reminded of the psychic toll, memories to haunt her.

These terms illuminate Pavlichenko's technical, psychological and moral challenges. They help us see her not just as a marksman but as a human grappling with enormous choices and burdens. As we follow her journey, this lexicon will guide us, reminding us of the path from student to sniper, the dilemmas she navigated that defined her legacy.

First Blood: The Trial by Fire

In the bitter winter of 1941, on the outskirts of Odessa, young Lyudmila prepared to take her first life. The 24-year-old student turned sniper had been thrust into the crucible of war. Nazi forces besieged the once bustling port city, and its defenders fought fiercely to hold the line. In this cauldron of fire and steel, Lyudmila would face her trial by fire - a harrowing initiation that would test her resolve and shape her legend.

Weeks earlier, Lyudmila arrived at the front lines as one of many fresh-faced recruits rushed to bolster Odessa's defenses. She excelled in her training, demonstrating a natural aptitude for marksmanship that caught the eye of her commanders. Yet theory and practice differed vastly. As she took her position in a shattered factory overlooking enemy lines, the weight of real combat settled heavily upon her shoulders.

The factory lay in ruins, its walls pockmarked by shelling and its windows blown out by explosions. It offered a commanding view but little protection from the biting cold or enemy guns. Lyudmila nestled into her carefully prepared hideout amid the rubble, having spent hours piling debris to break up her silhouette and draping camouflage netting to blend into the shadows.

As she peered through her rifle scope, scanning enemy positions, the reality of her task sank in. These weren't paper targets or wooden silhouettes - they were living, breathing men with families and dreams. The thought made her hands tremble and her breath catch. Could she really take a life? Could she bear that burden?

Lyudmila took a deep breath. She had drilled these principles countless times, etching them into muscle memory: accounting for crosswinds with windage, arcing the bullet over distance with elevation, and leading the shot to hit a moving target.

Her target came into focus. Curling her finger around the trigger, Lyudmila stilled her racing heart. The world narrowed to this singular moment. Breathe in. Aim. Breathe out. Fire.

In the Crosshairs: Sniper Vs. The World

Lyudmila Pavlichenko was the epitome of a silent yet deadly Soviet sniper during World War 2. Though young and once a student, she became a hardened sharpshooter. Her journey from recruit to veteran during the Siege of Odessa highlighted her remarkable skill and the unique challenges she faced as a woman on the male-dominated battlefield.

To understand Lyudmila's extraordinary career, we must examine the context of her foes and contemporaries. Elite snipers like Simo Häyhä, Matthäus Hetzenauer, and Vasily Zaitsev racked up hundreds of kills. They patiently waited for the perfect shot, sowing chaos among enemy ranks as unseen predators. Lyudmila endured the same brutal conditions - bone-chilling cold, the threat of counter-sniper fire, and the psychological toll of intimate killing.

Yet Lyudmila faced additional adversity as a woman in a male military. Less than 3% of the Red armies combat personnel were women. She battled skepticism, harassment, and discrimination from her own side. Female soldiers were often viewed as temporary wartime necessities rather than skilled warriors. Lyudmila had to be exceptional - her actions beyond reproach, her aim true and lethal. Each kill shattered preconceptions about her competence.

This pressure forged resilience in Lyudmila. Her first kills in Odessa earned her sniper's stripes. But the true crucible was the siege of Sevastopol, where she cemented her legend. For 250 grueling days, she haunted the rubble-strewn streets, turning every window into a threat. She honed her skills to ruthless perfection - patience, icy calm, and a killer's instinct.

Lyudmila's tally grew day by day. 100 kills. 200. 250. The Germans, once disdainful of a female sniper, now whispered her name in fear as the "Lady Death." Her legendary precision and femininity made her an object of grim fascination.

Yet this outward legend contrasted with her inward humanity. Taking life, even an enemy's, chips away at the soul. Lyudmila grappled with the immense burden and emotional toll, sharing this weight with snipers of all genders and nations.

This complexity makes Lyudmila's story compelling. She was not a mere killing machine but a person torn by the dark contradictions of her role. While united with all snipers in this struggle, she also stood apart, excelling in a man's world. Every kill cracked the glass ceiling, proving that the elite sniper's qualities transcend gender.

Today, as more women integrate into combat roles, Lyudmila's legacy gains new resonance. She was a trailblazer proving patience, precision, and fortitude know no gender. Her story reminds us of the sacrifices made by those who kill to save others - and the humanity behind the crosshairs.

CHAPTER 2: THE SNIPER'S DILEMMA

A sniper's world is a solitary one, filled with long stretches of isolation interrupted by brief moments of intense action. It's a realm where the line between hunter and hunted blurs, and taking lives can crush the spirit. Lyudmila Pavlichenko faced this stark reality daily as a Soviet sniper during World War II. From the rubble-strewn streets of Odessa to the hellscape of Sevastopol, she grappled with the unique physical and psychological challenges of being a sniper.

The physical demands were grueling. Snipers must remain motionless for hours or even days, waiting for the perfect shot. They endure biting cold, searing heat, hunger, thirst, and constant enemy fire. Lyudmila had to master her body, controlling every twitch and breath, becoming as still and silent as the grave. The slightest movement could give away her position, inviting a lethal response.

But the psychological toll was perhaps even heavier. Snipers engage in the most intimate form of killing, seeing their victim's faces through the scope and watching the life drain away. Each kill, no matter how justified, chips away at the soul. Lyudmila had to compartmentalize, separating the act from the person, or risk being crushed by the weight of her actions.

The solitude compounded this burden. Snipers often operate alone or in small teams, isolated from the camaraderie of regular troops. Lyudmila spent countless hours alone with her thoughts, replaying each kill and questioning her actions. In the silence, the mind can become its own worst enemy, conjuring doubts and demons.

If left unchecked, these pressures could break even the strongest warrior. Snipers who lost their psychological edge became a liability. They hesitated at critical moments, missed shots, or snapped under the strain. Lyudmila knew she had to find strategies to maintain her focus and sanity.

Sight Alignment: Understanding the Sniper's Focus

A novice shooter wonders, "What if I shoot and miss the target?" In the demanding world of long-range precision shooting, there's no room for error or second chances. One small mistake can spell catastrophic mission failure instead of a clean kill.

This is where sight alignment comes into play. It

refers to precisely aligning the firearm's front and rear sights with the shooter's eye. When these three elements form a straight line pointing at the target, the weapon is properly aligned. This foundational principle underpins all precision shooting.

The concept of sight alignment traces back to the earliest firearms. As soon as humans attached sights to weapons for aiming, the importance of lining them up became clear. Whether a basic front blade sight on a flintlock musket or sophisticated modern optics, the core idea remains the same: align the sights to align the shot.

But sight alignment is more than just lining up metal pieces. It's a mindset, a philosophy - an unwavering commitment to perfection where millimeters matter. For the sniper, mastering it isn't just a useful skill but a way of life.

Elite snipers spend countless hours honing their craft, ingraining sight alignment principles so deeply into muscle memory that it becomes instinct. Through relentless training, they develop an almost preternatural ability to align under the most adverse conditions imaginable.

In the heat of battle, with their heart pounding and adrenaline surging, a sniper must calm their breathing, steady their hand, and align with machine-like precision. There is no "close enough" - only the perfect alignment to drop the target with one round. Anything less is unacceptable.

To achieve this level of precision, snipers develop superhuman focus and discipline. They train themselves to tune out all distractions and pour their entire being into aligning those sights. This single-minded focus is often called "getting into the bubble" - a meditative state where only the sniper, rifle, and target exist.

Within this bubble, the complexities of ballistics still apply, but they are secondary to sight alignment. A sniper could make perfect windage and elevation adjustments, but a fraction of misalignment at the critical moment will send the shot wide.

This is why sniper schools worldwide drill sight alignment as the cardinal rule: breathe, relax, aim, align, and squeeze the trigger - repeat until it becomes instinct. Because in the field, there may only be one chance to take the shot and one fleeting moment when the target lines up.

In that critical instant, the sniper's entire existence narrows to aligning front sight, rear sight, and eye in perfect harmony. For that eternal second, their focus is absolute - mind and body locked in synchronicity, united in pursuit of one perfect shot across vast distances.

And when those sights align and that perfect sight picture crystallizes, the sniper exhales one final breath and squeezes the trigger with a gentle, loving pull. The rifle recoils, the round flies downrange, and the target drops. The shot is good.

This is the essence of a sniper's craft - not flashy showmanship, but the quiet, unshakable discipline of aligning sights and breaking the shot with inhuman consistency and precision, again and again.

To understand the sniper's mind is to look at the basic act of sight alignment, where their focus begins and ends. Everything else - the terrain, weather, tactics - matters, but is secondary to the imperative of putting sights on target.

A sniper enamored with accessories over marksmanship fundamentals will soon miss shots. And in their world, a miss is as good as a death sentence for themselves, their team, and the mission.

So they train relentlessly to make alignment as instinctive as breathing, etching it into their subconscious as a mantra, a prayer, a reason for being. Line up the front sight, rear sight, and shooter's eye, then let fly. Simple on paper, but executing with consistency under immense combat pressure requires focus and fortitude few possess.

That's what makes snipers a breed apart - not just elite soldiers, but zen masters of the art of alignment. Their focus is their greatest weapon, more lethal than any rifle. And it all distills down to those tiny pieces of metal and the aiming eye behind them, working in perfect unison to deliver death with pinpoint precision.

Sight alignment is more than a technique - it's a window into the sniper's soul. To witness them at work, aligning their shot amidst overwhelming chaos, is to glimpse the very essence of human focus and determination. A terrible beauty - the sniper's dance of death, performed one perfect alignment at a time until the last target falls. This is the sniper's purest art form.

Front sight, rear sight, shooter's eye. Align, focus, destroy. The sniper's focus is absolute.

Through the Scope: A Sniper's History

From the earliest days of firearms, the idea of precision shooting over long distances captivated military strategists and changed warfare. The history of sniping takes us on a fascinating journey, tracing how marksmanship, tactics, and technology evolved into this deadly art. To truly grasp the sniper's role, we must look back through history's scope at this specialized combat form's origins.

Sniping's origins trace back to the 16th century with the first accurate long-range firearms. In 1594, an English soldier named John Dyke recorded the first known sniper shot. He used a matchlock musket to shoot a Spanish soldier from an astonishing 300 yards away - a near-miraculous feat given firearms' primitive state back then.

As firearms advanced over the centuries, so did

precision shooting concepts. In the American Revolutionary War, skilled "riflemen" used the technologically advanced long rifle to harass British troops from afar. These early frontier snipers proved devastatingly effective, able to pick off officers and disrupt troop movements.

The Napoleonic Wars brought further rifle advancements like the Baker rifle, more accurate than smoothbore muskets. Specialized riflemen units like the 95th Rifles and Green Jackets worked as skirmishers and sharpshooters, disrupting enemy formations and eliminating high-value targets.

Sniping truly emerged as a powerful battlefield tactic during the American Civil War. The rifled musket greatly increased infantry weapon range and accuracy, allowing skilled marksmen to hit targets at previously unheard-of distances. Many rural Confederate soldiers who were skilled hunters proved particularly adept snipers, using superior marksmanship to devastating effect against Union troops.

One famous Confederate sniper was Jack Hinson, a 57-year-old farmer who took up arms after Union soldiers executed his two sons. Using a custom .50-caliber rifle, Hinson wreaked havoc, picking off over 100 soldiers with impunity from concealed spots.

World War I saw further sniping tactic and technology advances. With trench warfare, snipers played a crucial stalemate role on the Western Front. Using specialized rifles with telescopic sights, snipers staked out no man's land positions, patiently waiting for exposed enemy soldiers. Top snipers like Francis Pegahmagabow and Matthias Hetzenauer racked up hundreds of confirmed kills.

Sniping reached its peak during World War II, as advancements in rifle technology, camouflage, and tactics combined to create a new breed of highly trained, specialized soldiers. Snipers proved crucial on all fronts from the Eastern Front steppes to Pacific jungles.

Famous WWII snipers include the Soviet Lyudmila Pavlichenko with 309 kills, and Finnish Simo Häyhä with over 500 kills against the Soviets. Using patience, stealth, and incredible marksmanship, these elite soldiers terrorized enemy forces and turned battles.

Since WWII, sniping continued evolving with better rifle technology, optics, and ballistics making snipers deadlier than ever. In Vietnam's jungles, American and Vietnamese snipers engaged in a deadly game, with skilled marksmen wreaking havoc. Legendary U.S. Marine Carlos Hathcock recorded over 90 kills, including an astonishing 2,500-yard shot that remained the longest confirmed kill until 2002.

In recent Iraq and Afghanistan wars, snipers played a critical counterinsurgency role, providing overwatch for troops on the ground. With high-tech systems like the CheyTac M200 and Barrett M82, snipers can now engage targets over 2,000 meters away with incredible accuracy.

Despite technological advances, a sniper's core skills remain timeless: patience, discipline, and unwavering commitment to perfection. Sniping's history testifies to these elite soldiers' incredible skill and fortitude, who shaped warfare's course through precision and resolve.

From firearms' earliest days to modern 21st century battlefields, the sniper remained a constant, silent, and deadly force capable of changing history with one well-placed shot. By looking through history's scope, we gain deeper appreciation for this fascinating, deadly art and those who practice it.

The Sniper's Truth: Separating Myth From Reality

Legendary stories often overshadow reality, especially for professions shrouded in secrecy like snipers. No one has been more mythologized than Lyudmila Pavlichenko, the Soviet sharpshooter credited with 309 confirmed kills during World War II. To truly appreciate her achievements, we must separate myths from facts and examine evidence.

The main claim is that Pavlichenko was the most successful female sniper in history with 309 kills. This figure comes from official Soviet military records. As a Red Army sniper, Pavlichenko's kills were meticulously logged and confirmed by witnesses per military standards, lending credibility to the count. Contemporary Soviet and Western media accounts during the war also corroborate this kill count and show she was a skilled, dedicated sniper.

Some historians doubt the reliability of Soviet records, suggesting inflated numbers for propaganda. However, no evidence indicates Pavlichenko's tally was exaggerated. The consistency between official records, contemporary accounts, and Soviet verification processes strongly suggests 309 kills is accurate.

Beyond the number, firsthand accounts reveal Pavlichenko's careful approach to sniping. She studied the battlefield, used camouflage, remained calm, and precisely hit moving targets. Her reputation as the "unseen terror" shows her psychological impact on enemies. Her high kill count also demonstrates her effectiveness at disrupting enemy operations.

Contrary to myth, Pavlichenko did not operate alone. Like most snipers, she worked closely with a spotter who located targets, judged distances, and watched for counter-sniping threats. Claims that she primarily targeted officers also lack evidence, as most of her confirmed kills were likely regular infantry.

In conclusion, records and firsthand accounts

strongly support Pavlichenko as the most successful female sniper of World War II with 309 confirmed kills. Her skill, tactics, and psychological impact highlight her effectiveness. While myths surround her legend, her true legacy lies in the facts of her remarkable, dedicated service and the standard she set for snipers.

CHAPTER 3: WHO FEARED LYUDMILA PAVLICHENKO?

Lyudmila Pavlichenko's name struck terror into the hearts of her adversaries during World War II. As the most successful female sniper in history, she became a legend on the battlefields. Her skill, courage, and determination made her a formidable force that all enemies feared.

Why did Pavlichenko inspire such dread? We must look at her impact on the front lines to understand. Her reputation preceded her. The mere whisper of her presence sent shivers down soldiers' spines. Pavlichenko's victims never saw their fate coming. A single bullet from her rifle meant a swift, merciless death. This created an atmosphere of constant paranoia among German ranks.

Many believed Pavlichenko's prowess was just Soviet propaganda. They couldn't fathom a woman capable of such deadly accuracy and resolve. Witnessing her skills firsthand shattered their illusions, leaving them vulnerable to fear's crippling grip.

Pavlichenko's legend grew with each confirmed kill. Stories of her exploits spread like wildfire, awe-inspiring yet deeply unsettling. Soldiers began attributing fallen comrades' deaths to her, fueling the mythos surrounding this single sniper's power over battles. Failed attempts to eliminate her only strengthened her legend and terror.

Pavlichenko waged psychological warfare, sowing doubt, uncertainty, and fear to erode enemy morale. Soldiers became hesitant to expose themselves, fearing it could be their last moment. This hesitation often led to mistakes, giving Soviet forces advantages. Her presence symbolized Soviet resilience, inspiring comrades while striking fear into enemies.

Her legend infected enemy ranks like a virus. Soldiers whispered Pavlichenko's name, wondering if they would be next. The fear transcended battlefields, infiltrating the enemy's core psyche. Each kill added to her status as a formidable, terrifying opponent – a blow to their pride in facing a single Soviet woman's devastating losses.

The fear Pavlichenko inspired proved a powerful weapon. It demoralized enemies, sapped fighting spirit, and eroded confidence in victory. Her legend burdened their minds, creating an uncertain climate favoring Soviet forces.

Pavlichenko's impact extended beyond individual achievements. She became defiance, resilience, and unbreakable Soviet spirit personified. The terror she caused testified to her skill and courage – one woman's profound difference against overwhelming odds. As we remember her legacy, we recognize her psychological impact and the strength within each of us to inspire terror through dedication and unparalleled ability.

The Siege of Sevastopol: A Sniper's Playground

The Siege of Sevastopol was a pivotal moment in Lyudmila Pavlichenko's legendary career. This harrowing 8-month battle showcased her unparalleled sniping skills and cemented her place in history. Let's explore the strategies and challenges she faced while adapting the sniper's creed of marksmanship, stealth, and patience to emerge victorious against all odds.

In 1941, the crucial Soviet naval base of Sevastopol on the Black Sea came under intense German assault. Hitler unleashed the full might of his forces, determined to neutralize the Soviet threat. Amid this chaos, the young Pavlichenko, barely in her 20s, arrived to defend her homeland. Little did the Germans know they were about to face a formidable foe who would become their living nightmare.

Pavlichenko confronted the sheer scale and

intensity of the German onslaught as her primary challenge. Soviet defenders, outnumbered and outgunned, faced relentless bombardments, air raids, and infantry assaults threatening to overwhelm their positions at any moment. For a sniper like her, this meant constantly shifting firing positions, adapting to the ever-changing battlefield, and seizing fleeting opportunities to strike.

Pavlichenko mastered the sniper's art. She embodied marksmanship, honing her skills until each shot found its mark with unerring precision. Her stealth allowed her to move like a ghost through the rubble-strewn streets, always one step ahead of the enemy. And her patience was legendary - she could wait motionless for hours, even days, for the perfect moment to pull the trigger.

One incident showcased her incredible skills and determination. During a fierce firefight, a German sniper who had already claimed several Soviet lives pinned her down. For three days, they engaged in a deadly game of cat and mouse, each trying to outmaneuver the other. Pavlichenko's patience and discipline finally paid off - in a moment of perfect alignment, she fired a single shot that found its mark, eliminating the threat and saving countless lives.

Throughout the siege, Pavlichenko racked up an astonishing tally - 309 confirmed kills, including 36 enemy snipers. Her actions eliminated key German targets but also struck a powerful psychological blow. The mere mention of her name spread fear and uncertainty among German ranks, eroding their morale and combat effectiveness.

But Pavlichenko's impact went beyond the battlefield. Soviet propaganda spread her story, and she became a symbol of Soviet resilience and determination, a hero for a nation under siege. Here was a young woman, barely out of her teens, standing toe-to-toe with the might of the German war machine and emerging victorious.

Pavlichenko's success holds valuable lessons. It demonstrates the critical importance of adaptability, adjusting tactics and approaches to shifting battlefield conditions. It highlights the psychological dimension of warfare, how a single individual can strike fear into the enemy's hearts. And it underscores the enduring power of the sniper's creed - marksmanship, stealth, and patience can overcome even the most formidable odds.

Some might argue that Pavlichenko's achievements were exaggerated for propaganda purposes or that her impact was overstated. But the historical record is clear - her actions played a crucial role in Sevastopol's defense, tying down German forces and buying time for Soviet reinforcements. Her tally of 309 confirmed kills stands as a testament to her skill and lethal efficiency.

In the end, the Siege of Sevastopol stands as a defining moment in Pavlichenko's career and sniping history. It demonstrated the devastating psychological impact a single sniper could have on enemy forces. When mastered and applied by a legend like Pavlichenko, the principles of the sniper's creed could turn the tide of battle. Her actions echo through the decades, a timeless testament to skill, bravery, and the unbreakable human spirit in the face of overwhelming odds.

Sniper Vs. Sniper: Battle of the Shadows

During World War II, Soviet and Nazi sharpshooters engaged in a deadly game of cat-and-mouse on the battlefield. On the surface, these elite marksmen shared similarities - patience, exceptional marksmanship, and icy calm. However, fundamental differences in ideology, training, and tactics shaped their contrasting roles.

We must first examine the context in which Soviet snipers operated. Hitler's armies surged across the Soviet border in a devastating blitzkrieg during Operation Barbarossa. Facing annihilation, the Soviet Union mobilized every citizen for total war and survival. Soviet snipers emerged as a potent force in these desperate times.

Often drawn from experienced hunters and marksmen, the Soviets hastily trained their snipers and thrust them into battle. They learned their deadly trade on the job, honing skills like stealth, patience, and iron discipline. They stalked rubble-strewn streets and shattered fields, always seeking the perfect shot.

In contrast, the Nazi sniper corps evolved from the elite Jäger regiments' reconnaissance and skirmishing traditions. Between the world wars, the Germans refined and codified rigorous marksmanship training and fieldcraft. When war erupted in 1939, their sniper schools produced highly trained, technically proficient marksmen with the finest equipment.

In the war's early years, German snipers decimated enemy officers, NCOs, and machine gun crews with chilling efficiency. However, as the bloody Eastern Front stalemate dragged on, the differences between Soviet and Nazi snipers became stark.

The Soviets adapted, improvising techniques like "snap shooting" at fleeting targets due to shortages of precision rifles and optics. They honed camouflage and concealment skills to survive the unforgiving no-man's-land. Meanwhile, the Germans remained specialized elites, deploying in small teams to carefully prepare "hides" for surgical strikes before melting away.

These contrasting approaches reflected deeper differences in how the sides waged war. For the Soviets, sniping was part of a larger "cult of the sharpshooter" with citizen soldiers defending the motherland. Snipers like Vasily Zaitsev and Lyudmila Pavlichenko became celebrated national heroes. For the Germans, sniping fit their clinical, hierarchical war doctrine of specialist strikes against command and control.

Ultimately, the battle between these snipers was decided by the larger sweep of history. As the tide turned against the Nazis after Stalingrad and Kursk, their sniper corps struggled defensively against the relentless Soviet advance. The Soviets, having adapted over years of brutal combat, excelled at infiltration and counter-sniping to ruthlessly neutralize their German counterparts.

The stories of these dueling snipers offer a fascinating lens into the Eastern Front's larger history - how differing military cultures and traditions collided in a battle of skill, will, adaptation, and attrition. The Soviet approach of mass participation, improvisation, and grit proved decisive against an enemy once deemed invincible.

Today, these snipers' exploits live on in military lore and popular culture, celebrated in various media. Yet their enduring contribution lies in lessons about warfare's nature - the primacy of adaptability, individual skill and will's power, and the thin line snipers walk between hunter and hunted. Their ghosts will continue whispering secrets to those following their deadly footsteps as long as conflicts rage.

The Unseen Terror: Spreading Fear Behind Lines

Among the harrowing experiences of WWII's

Eastern Front, few were as psychologically terrifying as the unseen threat of enemy snipers. Soldiers on both sides lived in constant fear of these hidden marksmen. This was especially true for German forces, who faced an increasingly skilled and deadly Soviet sniper corps as the war progressed. It wasn't just the physical danger of being shot that was the problem. It was the constant psychological burden of knowing an unseen enemy could strike at any moment.

The sniper threat had immense implications. Snipers could pin down entire units, disrupt operations, and erode morale. They targeted officers and specialists, sowing chaos and confusion. For individual soldiers, the fear was relentless. Every movement risked being their last. Every shadow concealed a threat. This pervasive fear led to paralysis, poor decisions, and the breakdown of unit cohesion and effectiveness.

If left unchecked, snipers could have severely hampered German operations and hastened their defeat. Imagine units refusing to move, vital missions failing, and fear spreading like a contagion through the ranks. In the high-stakes Eastern Front battle, such outcomes were catastrophic for Germany's war effort.

The Soviets recognized snipers' potential as psychological warfare weapons, not just tactical assets. They found the perfect embodiment in Lyudmila Pavlichenko. Pavlichenko wasn't just a skilled marksman; she became a living legend whose name struck fear into German soldiers' hearts.

Soviet propaganda actively cultivated Pavlichenko's fearsome reputation. Her exploits filled Soviet media while German troops whispered her name in hushed tones. She became a spectral figure who could appear anytime, anywhere. This amplified her psychological impact on the battlefield.

Beyond her actions, Pavlichenko symbolized Soviet resistance. She was a heroic figure inspiring her comrades while demoralizing enemies. Her legend spread uncertainty among German troops, making them question safety even far from the front. This strategic use of fear was psychological warfare's masterstroke.

Implementing this required coordination. Soviet outlets tirelessly spread stories of Pavlichenko's exploits, real and embellished. Snipers like her planned missions for maximum psychological effect, given freedom by Soviet commanders who recognized "fear missions"' value.

The results were palpable. German soldiers grew paranoid and wary, diminishing their effectiveness from constant sniper fear. Pavlichenko's name became a death curse. Some reports claim German units refused deployments where she was rumored. This fear factor significantly contributed to Soviet victories like Stalingrad and Kursk.

Other solutions like counter-snipers or protection

could have mitigated the threat somewhat, but reactively. They addressed symptoms, not causes. By weaponizing fear itself, the Soviets struck at German morale's heart.

Ultimately, Pavlichenko proved fear could be as potent as any rifle. Turning snipers' psychological impact into strategy was an invaluable Soviet contribution. Her legend reminds us of psychological warfare's power and the unseen battle for hearts and minds. Her story shows the most dangerous threats are often the unseen ones.

Understanding Sniping: More Than Just Pulling the Trigger

Have you ever wondered about the incredible skill and mental fortitude required to be a sniper? It's not just about pointing and shooting. Sniping is a demanding art and science that requires a rare combination of abilities, patience, and nerves of steel.

The primary objective of a sniper is to deliver precise fire on high-value targets from concealed positions at long ranges while minimizing the risk of detection. But this simple definition doesn't convey the true depth of the sniper's craft.

To succeed, snipers must master several critical skills. First is marksmanship - consistently hitting targets at extreme distances. They must have an intimate understanding of ballistics and account for factors like gravity, wind, humidity, and even the

Earth's rotation. They read wind patterns from the slightest movements of leaves and grass. One small miscalculation, and the shot could miss by inches or yards.

Before taking the shot, snipers employ exceptional fieldcraft to get into position undetected. They become masters of camouflage and concealment, blending seamlessly into the environment. Inch by painstaking inch, they crawl through brush and undergrowth, careful not to disturb vegetation. Their ghillie suits and rifle coverings must mimic the surrounding foliage and mask any shine or reflections.

Then comes the agonizing wait. Snipers maintain absolute stillness for hours or days, ignoring hunger, thirst, discomfort, and the call of nature. Through high-powered scopes, they patiently observe the target area. Any lapse in stealth - a scope glint or muzzle flash - risks exposing their position to devastating counter-fire.

The mental strain is immense. Snipers constantly second-guess tactics, calculations, and hide sites. They grapple with the psychological burden of taking lives. Training replicates the brutal stress of combat through battle sounds and artillery simulators, conditioning snipers to maintain composure under duress. Only those with exceptional discipline and emotional control can thrive amid such unrelenting tension.

A Timeline of Terror: Pavlichenko's Path

Lyudmila Pavlichenko's journey from promising student to feared sniper is truly extraordinary. This timeline charts her incredible transformation and the key kills that cemented her status as history's most successful female sniper.

1937: Pavlichenko, born in 1916 in Bila Tserkva, Ukraine, moved to Kiev at age 21 to work in an arms factory. She developed an interest in shooting and joined a local club, quickly impressing instructors with her natural skill and determination.

June 1941: When Nazi Germany invaded the Soviet Union, the 24-year-old Pavlichenko, then a history student at Kiev University, enlisted in the Red Army. She requested infantry and became a lethal sniper in the 25th Rifle Division, overcoming initial skepticism.

August 1941: Pavlichenko saw her first action defending Odessa. Her exceptional marksmanship and composure under fire earned respect and struck fear into the Germans. She recorded her first confirmed kills of officers and soldiers with chilling precision.

October 1941: As the Red Army fell back to Sevastopol in Crimea, Pavlichenko's sniper skills became instrumental. She racked up an astonishing tally, including 36 enemy snipers killed in duels. The Germans nicknamed her "Lady Death" as she picked off their ranks.

June 1942: Pavlichenko engaged in her most famous duel against a highly skilled German sniper who had claimed several Soviets. After three tense days of trying to lure each other into a mistake, she outwitted him with a brilliant feint, putting a bullet through his head.

July 1942: After brutal months of fighting and being wounded, Pavlichenko left the front with 309 confirmed kills, including 36 snipers - making her the most successful female sniper ever. She received the Soviet Union's highest honor, the Gold Star of the Hero.

Late 1942: Pavlichenko's prowess led Soviet leaders to send her on a publicity tour to rally Allied support. She became the first Soviet citizen welcomed at the White House by President Roosevelt, drawing huge crowds fascinated by her story.

1943-1945: Back home, Pavlichenko transitioned to training the next generation of Soviet snipers, men and women, passing on her deadly skills.

Post-War: After finishing her education at Kiev University, Pavlichenko became a historian. Her memoirs "Lady Death" offer insight into one of history's deadliest snipers. She remained a revered symbol of Soviet resolve and skill.

From those first 1941 shots to her final 1942 tally, Lyudmila Pavlichenko blazed a trail of courage and skill rarely equaled. Her transformation from citizen to sniper to hero stands as a testament to her sheer grit. Each kill, each duel, built the portrait of a true warrior whose skill and spirit turned the tide of war. Her career timeline is a roadmap of resilience, showing how one person's resolve can inspire generations to face challenges head-on, like the legendary Lady Death.

The Proof in the Propaganda: Myth Vs. Reality

Lyudmila Pavlichenko captured people's imagination with her incredible accomplishments as a sniper during World War II. She confirmed 309 kills, elevating her to legendary status. However, like many wartime heroes, the line between fact and fiction often blurs, especially with propaganda's fog.

The Soviet Union was not immune to embellishing stories for morale and PR during conflicts. Pavlichenko's impressive battlefield feats provided ample material for their propaganda machine. Her image as a deadly female sniper thriving in a male role was too good not to exploit.

Let's start with the facts about Pavlichenko's story. Records confirm she volunteered for the Red Army shortly after the German invasion in 1941. She had pre-existing shooting skills, and her superiors decided to utilize her talents as a sniper, a role she quickly proved worthy of.

Her involvement in defending Odessa and Sevastopol is well-documented. She racked up a significant portion of her confirmed kills during these intense battles. Her tally of 309 is staggering, making her the most successful female sniper in history. It included 36 enemy snipers, showcasing her skill in sniper duels.

With chilling precision, Pavlichenko picked off officers and soldiers, earning the nickname "Lady Death" from Germans. The famous three-day duel against a German sniper, which she reportedly won, is one of her story's more compelling but harder-to-verify elements.

After months of intense fighting and being wounded, Soviet leaders withdrew Pavlichenko from the front in 1942. Her impressive record led them to send her on a publicity tour in the United States to rally war effort support. She was the first Soviet citizen welcomed at the White House by President Roosevelt and drew large, fascinated crowds.

Upon returning to the Soviet Union, Pavlichenko transitioned into a training role, passing her skills to the next sniper generation. After the war, she finished her education and became a historian. Her memoirs, "Lady Death," offer insight into her experiences, though likely containing self-promotion.

The core facts about Pavlichenko's service are not in question: her voluntary enlistment, large confirmed kills number, status as the top female sniper, combat wounds, and post-war life. These accomplishments alone cement her place in history.

Soviet propaganda likely played up certain story aspects, and some dramatic tales may have been exaggerated or fabricated. But this does not diminish her actual battlefield achievements or war effort contributions.

Pavlichenko stepped up in a time of great need and excelled in a male role. She displayed incredible skill, courage, and resolve in unimaginable adversity. Her 309 confirmed kills represent 309 lives - sons, fathers, husbands - that she personally ended, a weight few can comprehend.

Pavlichenko's legacy rests on her significant battlefield impact and inspiration to fellow soldiers and countrywomen. She showed women were capable of not just serving in combat but being elite warriors.

The propaganda surrounding her, though embellished, served a noble purpose: boosting morale, giving hope, and celebrating a woman's rare accomplishments. If details were exaggerated, it highlighted a greater truth - Pavlichenko was a real hero who made a real difference.

As we look back, it's important to separate fact from fiction as much as possible without diminishing our appreciation for what she achieved. Hers is a story of skill, courage, and determination worth remembering and celebrating, myths and all.

The most fitting tribute is not obsessing over every fact versus fiction but remembering her as she was: a skilled sniper, brave soldier, trailblazer for women in combat, and true Soviet hero. That reality of Lyudmila Pavlichenko is worth celebrating.

CHAPTER 4: OTHER NOTABLE MENTIONS

Lyudmila Pavlichenko may lead the way when it comes to World War 2 heroics with a rifle, but that doesn't mean there weren't others that sought to match her prowess. Here we have three other notable female Soviet snipers during World War II who, like Lyudmila Pavlichenko, made significant contributions to the war effort:

Roza Shanina

Roza Shanina was born on April 3, 1924, in the village of Yedma in the Arkhangelsk region of the Soviet Union. From a young age, she exhibited a strong sense of determination and resilience. Roza aspired to further her education and worked diligently to overcome the economic hardships of her family, ultimately enrolling in a teacher training college.

When the German forces invaded the Soviet Union,

Shanina felt a deep sense of duty to defend her country. She joined the Vsevobuch program and later volunteered for the Red Army in 1943, where she received sniper training at the Central Women's Sniper Training School. Roza quickly demonstrated exceptional skill and precision with a sniper rifle.

Shanina was deployed to the front lines in the 184th Rifle Division. Her first confirmed kill came in April 1944, and she rapidly gained a reputation for her bravery and effectiveness. Shanina's tally of confirmed kills reached 59, including 12 during the Battle of Vilnius. Her courage was further exemplified during the East Prussian Offensive, where she often volunteered for dangerous missions. Tragically, she was killed in action on January 28, 1945, while shielding a wounded commander.

Roza Shanina was posthumously awarded the Order of Glory 3rd Class. Her diaries, which provide a poignant glimpse into her experiences and thoughts during the war, have been published and remain a testament to her bravery and the role of women in combat.

Nina Lobkovskaya

Nina Lobkovskaya was born on March 8, 1924, in the Altai Krai region of the Soviet Union. Growing up, she was determined and disciplined, qualities that would serve her well in her future military career. Nina's life took a dramatic turn when the war broke out and she felt compelled to join the fight against the invading forces. Lobkovskaya joined the Red Army in 1942 and underwent sniper training at the Central Women's Sniper Training School. Her natural aptitude for marksmanship and leadership quickly became evident, leading to her assignment as a sniper instructor before she was deployed to the front lines. Lobkovskaya served with distinction in several major battles, including the Battle of Berlin. As the commander of a female sniper company, she played a crucial role in eliminating enemy forces and providing critical support to advancing Soviet troops. Her leadership and bravery were instrumental in her unit's success, and she personally accounted for numerous confirmed kills.

After the war, Nina Lobkovskaya continued to serve in the military and was recognized for her contributions with numerous medals and honors. Her story remains an inspiring example of courage and dedication.

Aliya Moldagulova

Aliya Moldagulova was born on October 25, 1925, in the Kazakh SSR. Orphaned at a young age, she was raised by her uncle. Despite the hardships, Aliya was a determined and spirited individual, known for her strong will and determination to overcome adversity. Moldagulova joined the Soviet Army in 1942 and trained as a sniper at the Central Women's Sniper Training School. She was deployed to the front lines with the 54th Rifle Brigade, where her skills were quickly put to the test. Aliya participated in several key battles, and her marksmanship and bravery earned her a reputation as a formidable sniper. During the Novosokolniki Offensive in January 1944, she demonstrated exceptional valor. Despite being wounded, she continued to fight, leading an attack that resulted in the capture of a strategic position. Moldagulova's actions greatly contributed to the success of her unit, but she was fatally wounded during the battle.

Aliya Moldagulova was posthumously awarded the title Hero of the Soviet Union, the highest distinction for bravery in combat. Her story is celebrated in Kazakhstan and across the former Soviet Union as a symbol of courage and sacrifice.

These female snipers exemplify the significant contributions and bravery of Soviet women during World War II, challenging traditional gender roles and making an indelible mark on military history.

CHAPTER 5: COMPARISON WITH MODERN SNIPERS

Snipers, both in the era of World War II and in contemporary times, have played a crucial role in military operations. However, the challenges and conditions they faced are markedly different due to technological advancements, changes in military strategy, and variations in training methods. This comparative analysis looks at the trials experienced by WWII snipers, epitomized by Lyudmila Pavlichenko, and those confronted by modern-day snipers.

1. Training and Selection

During World War II, sniper training and selection processes were rudimentary compared to modern standards. Lyudmila Pavlichenko, for instance, was a university student who joined a paramilitary organization and learned shooting skills. The formal sniper schools that existed were basic, and the training focused primarily on marksmanship. The curriculum often included limited fieldcraft, camouflage, and basic stalking techniques. Training durations were short, often a few weeks, due to the urgent need for skilled snipers at the front. In contrast, modern sniper training is extensive and highly specialized. Modern snipers undergo rigorous selection processes to ensure they possess the necessary physical and psychological attributes. Training programs last several months and encompass a broad spectrum of skills including advanced marksmanship, fieldcraft, camouflage, intelligence gathering, and survival techniques. Modern snipers also receive training in using sophisticated equipment such as range finders, night vision devices, and advanced sniper rifles. The psychological training includes stress inoculation and scenarios designed to simulate the pressures of real combat situations.

2. Equipment and Technology

WWII snipers like Pavlichenko used relatively primitive equipment. Sniper rifles of the era, such as the Mosin-Nagant with a telescopic sight, lacked the precision and range of modern weapons. The scopes had fixed magnifications and were prone to fogging and damage. Ammunition quality was inconsistent, and snipers often had to account for significant variability in bullet performance.

Communication technology was also limited, often relying on field telephones and messengers, which could delay critical information. Today, snipers benefit from advanced technology that significantly enhances their effectiveness. Modern sniper rifles, such as the M40 or the Barrett M82, are designed for precision and have greater range and reliability. Scopes now offer variable magnification, laser range-finding, and are often equipped with ballistic computers that assist in making precise shots over long distances. Communication has been revolutionized with secure, real-time radio systems and satellite communication, enabling snipers to relay information and receive orders instantaneously. Additionally, modern ghillie suits and camouflage materials are more effective and adaptable to different environments.

3. Combat Conditions and Environment

WWII snipers operated in harsh and varied environments, often without the luxury of modern support systems. Pavlichenko, for instance, fought in the brutal conditions of the Eastern Front, dealing with extreme cold, snow, and limited supplies. Snipers had to remain in static positions for extended periods, facing the constant threat of artillery, tanks, and infantry assaults. The urban warfare in cities like Stalingrad introduced additional challenges of rubble, close-quarter engagements, and snipers from the enemy. Modern snipers operate in diverse environments, from urban settings to mountainous regions and deserts. However, they have access to better support in terms of logistics, medical evacuation, and intelligence. Advances in materials and technology have improved the survivability and comfort of snipers in harsh conditions. Modern warfare also often involves asymmetric threats, requiring snipers to engage in counter-insurgency operations, dealing with unconventional tactics used by irregular forces.

4. Psychological and Physical Demands

The psychological burden on WWII snipers was immense. They often operated alone or in pairs, isolated from their units for long periods. The constant threat of being discovered and targeted by enemy forces added to the stress. The brutality of the conflict, witnessing the deaths of comrades, and the sheer scale of the war had significant psychological impacts. Physical endurance was crucial, as snipers had to endure extreme weather conditions, long marches, and the rigors of prolonged engagements without adequate rest. While modern snipers also face significant psychological and physical demands, they benefit from better psychological support and medical care. Training programs emphasize mental resilience, and there is greater awareness of issues like PTSD, with support systems in place for those affected. Physically, modern snipers are equipped with better gear, including body armor, hydration systems, and nutrition plans to maintain peak physical condition. The use of advanced optics and spotting scopes has also reduced some of the physical strain associated with long-range observation.

5. Role and Tactical Employment

The role of snipers in WWII was primarily focused on taking out high-value targets such as enemy officers, machine gunners, and other snipers. They were often employed defensively, providing support during infantry engagements and acting as a force multiplier. Their presence on the battlefield was a significant psychological deterrent to enemy forces. In contemporary military operations, snipers play a versatile role. They are used not only for eliminating high-value targets but also for intelligence gathering, reconnaissance, and providing overwatch for ground troops. Modern snipers often work in conjunction with special operations forces, participating in complex missions that require precision and coordination. The integration of snipers into broader tactical and strategic plans reflects their importance in modern warfare.

6. Historical and Societal Context

Snipers like Lyudmila Pavlichenko operated in a historical context marked by total war, with entire nations mobilized for conflict. Pavlichenko herself became a symbol of Soviet resistance and a celebrated war hero. The societal impact of

WWII snipers was profound, with their stories often used for propaganda to boost morale and exemplify heroism. Today's snipers operate in a different societal context. While they are still highly respected and their skills are revered, the nature of modern conflicts, often limited engagements or counter-terrorism operations, means their actions are not as widely publicized. However, the stories of modern snipers, such as those in Iraq and Afghanistan, continue to capture public imagination and contribute to the narrative of modern military heroism.

Conclusion

The trials faced by snipers like Lyudmila Pavlichenko during World War II were characterized by rudimentary training, basic equipment, and extreme combat conditions, requiring immense physical and psychological resilience. Modern-day snipers, although facing their own set of rigorous challenges, benefit from advanced technology, comprehensive training, and better support systems. While the fundamental role of snipers as precision marksmen remains unchanged, the evolution of their equipment, training, and tactical employment reflects broader changes in military strategy and technology. The legacy of WWII snipers continues to inform and inspire the practices and ethos of contemporary sniping, ensuring that the lessons learned from past conflicts are not forgotten.

CONCLUSION: LADY DEATH'S LEGACY

Lyudmila Pavlichenko's legacy echoes long after World War II faded into history. Her impact goes beyond incredible sniper accomplishments. It resonates in military strategy, women's combat roles, and wartime heroism itself. This exploration uncovers timeless lessons and inspirations from the legendary "Lady Death's" life and career.

First, Pavlichenko shattered gender barriers in the male-dominated military combat world. Her success as a sniper challenged deep-seated notions about women's battlefield capabilities. At a time when women largely filled support roles, she proved gender posed no barrier to becoming an elite warrior. Her 309 confirmed kills stand as a testament to her lethal skill and precision, earning respect from comrades and enemies alike.

Pavlichenko's achievements opened doors for women in the Soviet military and sent ripples globally. Her U.S. publicity tour showcased to the world a woman excelling in a male role, planting seeds of change in societal perceptions. Her trailblazer legacy continues inspiring women in the military today, proving courage and prowess know no gender.

Beyond personal accomplishments, Pavlichenko's legacy elevated snipers' role in military strategy. Her devastating effectiveness demonstrated precision marksmanship's power to shape battlefields and demoralize enemy forces. The "Lady Death" name German troops used underscored the psychological impact one skilled sniper could wield.

Pavlichenko's exploits, particularly her famed sniper duel, showcased the unique blend of patience, discipline, and nerve this role required. Her legacy underscores sharpshooters' strategic value, capable of altering battles with one well-placed shot. Today's militaries worldwide recognize sniper units' importance, a testament to trailblazers like Pavlichenko.

Resilience and determination are core to Pavlichenko's enduring legacy. Her story shows unwavering resolve amid unimaginable adversity. From Odessa and Sevastopol front lines to sniper duels testing her limits, she embodied an unbreakable spirit. Even after multiple wounds, she returned to fight with renewed vigor, driven by deep love for country and comrades.

This resilience extended beyond the battlefield. Post-war, Pavlichenko pursued education, becoming a historian. Her "Lady Death" memoirs testify to her commitment to sharing experiences with the world.

Pavlichenko's legacy serves as a wellspring inspiring future generations. Her story resonates with timeless courage, sacrifice, and the power of human spirit to overcome incredible odds. She stands as a beacon for those facing battles in military service or everyday life.

Her legacy's impact shows in countless books, films, and documentaries continuing to explore her story. Each retelling introduces Pavlichenko to new audiences, ensuring her feats and indomitable spirit inspire across generations and borders.

Perhaps most intriguingly, Pavlichenko's legacy blurs truth and legend. The Soviet propaganda machine undoubtedly shaped her story, embellishing details and crafting a larger-than-life "Lady Death" image. Yet this mythologizing boosted morale, instilled hope, and celebrated a woman's remarkable wartime accomplishments.

In war's fog and memory's haze, separating fact from fiction eludes. But the broader truths her story represents may give her legacy enduring power - her skill, courage, and trailblazing spirit remain unassailable.

Ultimately, Lyudmila Pavlichenko's legacy transcends time and place. It speaks to universal human capacity for greatness amid adversity. It challenges us to break barriers, push perceived limits, and stand firm in convictions.

Reflecting on her story reminds us heroes aren't born, but forged in conflict and sacrifice's crucible. Pavlichenko's legacy calls us to embrace inner strength, rise to our time's challenges, and leave an indelible historical mark.

The echoes of "Lady Death" resound, a potent reminder of one individual's power to shape history's course. Pavlichenko's legacy testifies to the enduring human spirit and timeless courage, resilience, and determination values. It will continue inspiring generations - a beacon guiding through darkness and reminding us of the indomitable strength within us all.

Printed in Dunstable, United Kingdom